GRAMMAR NAZIS ARE NOT ALWAYS ~~RITE~~,
~~RIGHT~~, WRITE

BASED ON A WRITING COURSE I TAUGHT
THAT REPUDIATED MOST OF WHAT IS CON-
SIDERED PROPER FOR WRITING FICTION

OTHER NOVELS BY ROBERT K. SWISHER JR.

Historical Fiction: Trade and E-book
Published by Sunstone Press
The Land
Fatal Destiny

Contemporary Fiction: Trade and E-book
PUBLISHED BY SUNSTONE PRESS
How Far the Mountain
The Last Narrow Gauge Train Robbery
The Last Day in Paradise
Love Lies Bleeding
The Man From the Mountain

Literary: Out of Print
Published by Samisdat - Canada
American Love Story

Young Adult: Trade Only
Published by Echo Press California
The Weaver

Published by Sunstone Press
Only Magic

Humor: E-book only
Conversations With the Golf God

Released as E-books:
Bob Roosevelt Mystery Series – 4 novels
Hope
How Bridge McCoy Learned to Say I Love you
A Circle Around Forever

Satire: Trade and E-book
Published by Open Talon Press
Vent
Grammar Nazis Are Not Always ~~Rite~~, ~~Right~~, Write

Short stories in literary journals, newspaper work, articles in outdoor magazines.

Reviews by Publishers Weekly, Best Sellers, Library Journal, Midwest Book Review, and many others.

GRAMMAR NAZIS ARE NOT ALWAYS ~~RITE~~, ~~RIGHT~~, WRITE

by

Robert K. Swisher Jr.

Text copyright © 2017 Robert K. Swisher Jr.
All rights reserved

PUBLISHED BY
OPEN TALON PRESS

EDITED BY: LIZ GAIDRY
FORMATTED BY: SHARON BROWNLIE / JESSE GORDON
COVER DESIGNER: SHARON BROWNLIE
SPECIAL APPRECIATION TO: DOLLY

Part of this book is a work of fiction. For the fiction segments names, characters, places and incidents are either products of the author's imagination or are used fictitiously. Any resemblance to actual events, locales, or persons either living or dead, is entirely coincidental. Part of this work might be construed as non-fiction. If any of this book reminds you of yourself and you get offended by certain comments or remarks (corporations included since you are by law considered people) no harm, malice, libel, racism, discrimination, in any of the previous terms multitudes of forms and definitions, and any term that would come to mind by any other person, was intentionally intended either by me, my wife, my dog, my cat, my goldfish, my hanging plants, or any relative - this includes all and any life forms in the known and unknown universe that might share some of my DNA, and unknowingly, by either cosmic intervention, or a form of communication as yet unknown to mankind had anything to do with the writing of this book.

If you wish to use portions of this book for anything but reviews you must contact OPEN TALON PRESS or the author. Sorry, what can I say? We all know lawyers run the world.

First Edition
Printed in the United States of America

Library of Congress – In Publication Data
Swisher, Robert K. 1947-
    Grammar Nazis Are Not Always Rite, Right, Write: Robert K. Swisher Jr.
    Summary: A writing book that repudiates most of what is taught or
    deemed necessary when writing fiction
    ISBN: 978-0-9979096-1-6
    LCN: 2017908283

TABLE OF CONTENTS

Other Novels by Robert K. Swisher Jr...3
Dedication..9
Chapter One—Why I Am Qualified to Write This Book.....................13
Chapter Two—Definition of a Grammar Nazi.....................................27
Chapter Three—Famous Authors Who Ignored Traditional
   Grammar and Punctuation...33
Chapter Four—The Whole Truth and Nothing But the Truth
   About Writing Fiction..37
Chapter Five—Age Old Questions Concerning Writing......................43
Chapter Six—The Word 'JUST' and a Few Other Choice Words........49
Chapter Seven—Punctuation..57
Chapter Eight—Spelling...65
Chapter Nine—The Myth of Show Don't Tell....................................69
Chapter Ten—Write What You Know..73
Chapter Eleven—Merely For Fun...77
Chapter Twelve—Once Again in Case You Have Forgotten –
   You Cannot Teach How to Write Fiction.......................................81
Chapter Thirteen—The Secrets of Writing..85
Chapter Fourteen—Editors...89
Chapter Fifteen—Copyright..93
Chapter Sixteen—Royalties Both Traditional and Self Published
   and a Few Comments On Book Promotion...................................97
Chapter Seventeen—Query Letter, Synopsis, and All That Other
   Gut Wrenching Stuff..107
Chapter Eighteen—Contracts...113
Chapter Nineteen—To Self Publish or Not and Free-Books.............119
Chapter Twenty—Book Reviews and Trolls......................................127
Chapter Twenty One—Random Questions.......................................131
Chapter Twenty Two—What Makes a Fiction Book Popular............143
Chapter Twenty Three—In Summary...147
Chapter Twenty Four— In Closing...151
Notes..155

DEDICATION

For all those obsessed with writing fiction do not worry – you do not suffer alone

CREATIVITY IS NOT BEING AFRAID TO FAIL

CHAPTER ONE
WHY I AM QUALIFIED TO
WRITE THIS BOOK

and

SOME BORING AND NOT SO BORING FACTS ABOUT MY LIFE THAT DEPENDING ON YOUR OUTLOOK EITHER CURSED ME OR BLESSED ME INTO BECOMING A WRITER.

But first an explanation:

I AM POSITIVE THIS BOOK WILL OFFEND GRAMMAR NAZIS, PEOPLE OBSESSED WITH PUNCTUATION, AND MORE THAN ONE CREATIVE WRITING PROFESSOR. I CANNOT SAY I AM SORRY. AT TIMES YOU GET TOO PICKY AND FORGET ABOUT THE STORY.

This book is based on a creative writing course I taught at a small university in the 1980's. Because the course repudiated the majority of things the other English and Creative Writing Professors held as gospel truth they were constantly peeved off at me as to what they considered my disregard for the rules of English, grammar, and the art of writing fiction.

This is not always true, but it is my belief that when it comes to writing fiction many of the grammar and punctuation rules can and should be ignored. Also, written in stone statements like, write what you know, never end a sentence in a preposition, are more times than not pure hogwash. The Professors were also grudgingly jealous of me because none of them had placed a novel at the time and eight of my novels had been published. To further anger many English and Creative Writing Professors I think tenure is a joke, which has nothing to do with this book, but it does have a lot to do with the overpriced university system (I am talking about the United States.)

To my great satisfaction and enjoyment my students thoroughly enjoyed the course and its philosophies even though my writing requirements were rather tough, three 2,500 word stories for the first three weeks, followed by two rewrites a week. The final was a finished 1500 hundred word story. The lowest grade I gave was a C+. My grading system was based on effort. If people showed no effort or desire to participate I dropped them from class so they did not get an incomplete or I had to fail them. I tried my best to encourage each student to follow their own muse with their writing and not fall into the world of what everyone else decides or professes to be correct - even writers succumb to the desire to be part of the crowd - which, in my opinion, stifles the unique creativity within each of us. I will say with pride many of my students are now published by reputable presses. The rest have done what most people do who give up on a writing career – they either became alcoholics, some form of illegal substance addict, or teachers, a small percentage became alcohol and drug addicted teachers.

This is not a how to book. If you are searching for the secret on how to write a bestseller there are several million how to books on the market you can squander your money on but the truth of the matter is **FICTION WRITING CANNOT BE TAUGHT**, there is no one way – there is no completely right way – there are many, many, many, ways to write a story – you simply have to be brave enough to be **YOU** and not out of the fear of rejection succumb to the herd mentality. If you do not believe this from a not very famous writer such as I this was also said by Earnest Hemingway, who, if I remember correctly, wrote a few good books, many of which were slammed by stylist and people who seemed to know what a correct novel is – "sentences are too short, writes like a journalist, etc…etc…"

Although there is one fact that is always true on how to write a novel, maybe not a bestseller but at least to finish a novel – the fact is simply **DO IT.** There are no excuses although people who profess to be writers can come up with hundreds of excuses why they cannot finish their novel. It does not necessarily take an education or deep inspiration to write a book – it takes diligence and work. This is also true for short stories and poetry.

For forty-nine years and counting I have spent my entire writing career going against the grain of what most fiction writers think is necessary or proper. I have made a tough game tougher by writing fiction that may fit into a genre, but is not format. Of the thirty novels I have written, not counting six I discarded, sixteen, with hard work and luck, have been published by traditional presses, eight of these are still in print and three have been released as e-books, two were optioned for several years but were not turned into movies because no one could raise 50 million dollars even though I volunteered to kick in my life savings of $134.99. I have also indied nine e-books and have done far better with them (both for reviews and monetary) than my expectations even though my mastery of online promotion and acquiring a mailing list is far from being stellar. My novels range from young adult, historical fiction, mystery, contemporary, and satire. I have written for newspapers and outdoor magazines. I am listed in Young Contemporary Authors and Who's Who in the West. Several of my books have been put on tape and CD's for the Blind and Physically Handicapped - a non-profit organization for which I donated the requested books. Many of my books have received outstanding reviews by all the big reviewing magazines.

During my writing career I have signed good contracts, bad contracts, and so so contracts. I have been paid by presses and not been paid. I have had presses go bankrupt on me. I have been with crooked agents and good agents. I have been asked to write a novel on spec and then the company went out of business after I worked on the book for close to a year. Besides doing book signings in book stores, doing radio interviews, I have sold books in grocery stores by the cabbage, on library steps, going into a rodeo, art fairs, farmers markets, art galleries, concerts, shopping malls, car shows, and door to door. I know the writing game. I have learned it in the trenches. Some of what I have learned I hope to pass on to you and hopefully save you a little grief – as you know or will discover the writing game is not always nice.

My average grade in high school English was a D. My overall grade point average in high school was a low C. The only reason it was that high is because I did well in P.E. High school to me was an endless succession of boring months and useless information. I have never been good at spitting facts and to this day diagramming a sentence has never been of any use to me. I was also one of those kids that was never in the clique – did not want to be – and still do not want to be. Watching the real world to me is the best and most profound fiction there is – it has to be fiction because there is no way it can be real.

While in elementary school I wrote short stories and poems that I made into books with cardboard covers held together with staples. In high school I filled countless spiral note-books with short stories and ramblings and dreamed about the day I would see my books in book stores. I still have these early literary achievements. I read them every so often with a nostalgic smile, remembering how innocent and naive I was at the time concerning the writing business, or writing game as I now call it. They also remind me how fast the days pass.

From an early age on I have always been a reader. I firmly believe if you are going to be a writer you must read. I still have my childhood copy of **THE LITTLE ENGINE THAT COULD** by Watty Piper, the pen name of Arnold Munk**,** and read it at least once a year. I now read everything: history, chick lit, fantasy, biographies, westerns, science fiction, end of the world, romance, literary, contemporary, mysteries, not much erotica - let's get real, there are only so many ways to do it and a limited number of words to describe the male and female anatomy before it starts to get ridiculous – she fondled his fly rod while he unbuttoned her blouse to expose two of the most majestic rainbow trout imaginable then they breathlessly tumbled into a frying pan of sensuous bacon grease – please, give me a break.

When I was younger I read books for the adventure and mystery. I became the story. I was the main character. I hated the villain. Now, I must confess, I read more to see how the author strings their words together, how they punctuate, their use of tense, sentence and paragraph structure, do they use the word **JUST**, do they use words ending in **ING** more than words ending in **ED**? Do they use more adverbs ending in **LY**? I decipher and analyze the book. In many ways it is sad but this is how it is. The only novel in many years that really swept me away solely for the story is: **A HUNDRED YEARS OF SOLITUDE** by Gabriel Marquez. For non-fiction it is **THE BOYS IN THE BOAT** by Daniel James Brown - the story of the boys on the Washington State rowing team who won the gold medal in the 1936 Olympics.

After high school I received a Masters of Life Degree as a radio operator with an infantry unit in Vietnam. In the army I learned life is random and controlled by luck. I also call it my love poetry stage, but, as things go, the object of my love poetry found waiting for a soldier too difficult. My love poetry ended up in a latrine – crapped on by hundreds of soldiers. Discharged from the army as a private - I was not really good at taking orders - I went to college on the G.I. Bill with the full intent of majoring in English and Creative Writing and becoming a fiction writer. I flunked out of college within a year and a half. College was nothing more than glorified high school and the rhetoric of the Creative Writing and English professors was boring and had nothing to do with the stories that were clamoring ruthlessly around in my head.

I must admit there are times when I read the credentials of some writers I am envious: Degree in Creative Writing with a masters in English Literature with a minor in Poetry Content of the Old Testament with another minor in the Greek masterpieces. Who cannot be impressed?

I did learn two things in college which have never left me: I do not trust the police (this was when cops and army units were killing college students) not that much different from now, and, I do not like semi-colons. You will never see a semi-colon in my work unless it was placed there by an editor and I missed removing it. I have been told by several writers using dashes in place of semi-colons is a sign of being an amateur. In a not so polite way I told them to _____ off. (Insert any word you think is appropriate)

During my brief college career I placed hundreds of poems and short stories with literary magazines. For each acceptance I was normally paid a dollar and a free copy, which did not cover the cost of the submission, but did make me feel like a true writer - I was published. These early works now rest in a trunk – their acid free paper slowly becoming yellow and brittle.

Out of college and feeling free for the first time in my life I rented a cheap one room apartment in a not so nice part of town - furnished it with a mattress and discarded furniture, bought a used Hermes typewriter, a book listing agents and small and large presses, and started writing a novel while continuing to send off short stories and poetry. Working at a fast food establishment kept me in stamps, envelopes, paper, ribbons, greasy salt enriched food, and cheap beer. I was in writer's heaven. Now, e-mail submissions are much cheaper and the wait for rejection is quicker – the greasy salt enriched food is even healthier.

To support my writing habit I have held numerous part time jobs. Here are a few: Worked on wheat harvest crew, a hog confinement center, farms, numerous bartending jobs, waiter, dishwasher, shoe salesman, door to door vacuum cleaner salesman, telemarketing everything from gold coins to adjustable beds to dental plans, car salesman, mowed yards, grocery store clerk, night shift at a convenience store, cowhand on a ranch, made windows in a window factory, built miles of fence, guided wilderness fishing trips, was a greens keeper at two golf courses, truck driver, milk man, taught a creative writing class not because of an education degree but based on my writing credentials, and a few jobs I am not really proud of but to my relief the statute of limitations has been surpassed. Now, in my senior years, and thanks to Social Security, Amazon, Barnes and Nobel, Nook Books, Kobo, Scribed, I books, several publishers, and my wife, I no longer have to worry about paying the bills, although I am far from being rich. My wife and I live a simple and enjoyable life.

If you do not have a passion for writing fiction please take my advice and do not waste your time reading this book. If you do have a passion for writing hopefully this book will give you the confidence to never give up. One of my best selling novels was rejected 400 times before it was accepted. It was the old days of paper submissions – 3 chapters, a synopsis, a query letter, and a stamped return envelope. None of the material could be photocopies. The book received numerous outstanding reviews and is still in print. In total I have received over 4,000 rejection letters. I used to save them but now with e-mail submissions I simply erase them and say to the blank screen, "Your loss," followed by a few other choice words.

Merely to strengthen your resolve to be a writer every writer should read: **ROTTEN REJECTIONS** edited by Andre Bernard – published by Pushcart Press. **ROTTEN REVIEWS** edited by Bill Henderson – published by Penguin Books. **A BOOK OF DAYS FOR THE LITERARY YEAR** edited by Neal T. Jones – published by Thames and Hudson.

If nothing else after you have read these when conversing about books at a literary party you will sound intelligent, although intelligence has nothing to do with writing fiction. Intelligence in many ways might get in the way.

I will warn you, you should not read more than two of the 4,238,951 thousand how to books covering proper grammar, sentence structure, tenses, and what not to do and do when writing a novel. They will leave you in a state of mass confusion and searching desperately to regain your own style. My only question about the majority of people who write how to write books is why have they not penned any real books? Real books in my opinion are novels.

CHAPTER TWO
DEFINITION OF A GRAMMAR NAZI

For their own safety the people who stated the following quotes will remain anonymous. I hold a deep fear that if they became known they and their entire family will be ruthlessly attacked by Grammar Nazis. I would not put it past a few Grammar Nazis to even attack the family bird for having bad vocabulary or the pet dog for barking out of tense. If you would like the names for the people who made the following quotes you may e-mail me, Facebook message me, or contact me on my web site, and I will send them to you. I will confess Number 8 is mine.

A GRAMMAR NAZI IS:

1) "A captious individual who cannot resist the urge to correct a spelling and or grammar mistake even in informal settings. After pointing out the linguistic shortcomings in others, a Grammar Nazi feels a strange sense of twisted and unconstructive intelligentsia delight."

2) "In reality, they are making someone else feel bad for no reason and unintentionally implying that their superior

grammar skills are all they have to show for a wasted liberal arts education."

3) "Please any and all of you Grammar Nazis – stick with formal writing and leave fiction writers alone – they have enough problems."

4) "If your book is attacked by a Grammar Nazi ignore it. There are very few perfect books. Now if the Grammar Nazi that attacks you has a halo and wings you might want to pay attention."

5) "To know and understand all the rules of grammar and punctuation is like saying you know and understand all the laws of the land. It is impossible."

6) "A person greatly hated or at the least despised for their superior attitude toward people without a masters degree in English."

7) "A person who has never once in their life misused there or their, too or to, I or me, later or latter, its or it's, toward or towards, a lot or alot, lay or lie, sit or sat, role or roll, dieing or dying, messed up tense one or two times in a 100,000 word manuscript, and heaven forbid never misspelled a word."

8) "One especially mean Grammar Nazi was my 12th grade English teacher who told me I could never be a writer if I did not correctly use semi-colons and learn how to diagram a sentence." Mrs. (last name withheld to protect the guilty) for your information if you are still alive, unless it is a mistake there is not one semi-colon in any of my published novels, short stories, numerous newspaper articles, hundreds of published poems, and I still cannot diagram a sentence nor do I wish to learn.

WRITE AND FORGET THE CONSEQUENCES

CHAPTER THREE
FAMOUS AUTHORS WHO IGNORED TRADITIONAL GRAMMAR AND PUNCTUATION

If you want more details about the following authors research them – you will find it interesting to say the least. If you are brave you can send quips to the Grammar Nazi of your choice. There are a many more famous authors who had a disdain for punctuation and grammar than are listed here but this book is not intended to be a who is who of the literary world that ignored convention.

1) E.E. Cummings: Harvard Graduate and veteran of WW I – used punctuation more as an art form and did more than rather well.

2) James Joyce: Read **ULYSES** and count the commas in the 256,000 word novel.

3) Cormac McCarthy: Will not use question marks and uses minimal punctuation – spells don't dont.

4) Jose Saramago: "Punctuation…is like traffic signs, too much of it distracts from the road on which you traveled."

5) Marcel Proust: 600 words long run-on sentence

6) William Faulkner: Read **THE SOUND AND THE FURY** – give it as a gift to your favorite Grammar Nazi.

7) Samuel Beckett: Wrote many works with no punctuation.

8) Junot Diaz: Does not like quotation marks.

9) Gertrude Stein: "Punctuation is necessary only for the feeble-minded."

10) Gabriel Marquez: Read any of his books – especially **NOBODY WRITES THE COLONEL**

THE HUNGER GAME novels were slammed for their punctuation and sentence structure. Also the **FIFTY SHADES OF GREY** series was lambasted by critics for its poor writing. In both cases this might be true, but in both cases the authors wrote the way they wanted, and now do not have to worry about paying the rent.

CHAPTER FOUR
THE WHOLE TRUTH AND NOTHING BUT THE TRUTH ABOUT WRITING FICTION

Every day agents and publishers around the world receive thousands and thousands of novel proposals. The average response time for a query is anywhere from two weeks to six months – this is for the agents and publishers that bother to respond – many now state you will not receive a response unless they are interested in reading more of your material. Their excuse being they are swamped by submissions and extremely busy. Gee thanks, that's big of you. I suppose you are the only people in the world who are extremely busy. I take it you feel writers are never busy – writing a book takes no effort at all – hell, I can write an 85,000 word book in a few days then I lay around and drink beer and let the novel edit itself.

The fortunate novel that does get published by a traditional publisher, either with the help of a busy agent or clawing its way through the slush pile, will be lucky if it sells two thousand copies. The slush pile is a query submitted without being asked – good agents receive 500 to a 1,000 a week.

On a normal year there are several million books self-published either through vanity presses or Amazon and its counterparts – only a handful will sell more than a few hundred copies.

There are hundreds of books that profess they will teach you how to write a best seller. If you believe this mail me $12.95 and I will teach you how to win the Lotto or go to Las Vegas and beat the house.

Welcome to the world of a fiction writer. This is not a career for the weak of heart or a person who cannot take rejection. Being a little crazy helps, also the consumption of alcohol. The ingestion of drugs does not unless it is copious amounts of coffee.

To be blunt your chances of making a living as a fiction writer, either through traditional channels or the self-publishing route, are somewhere in the range of ice cream being served in hell. Don't fret, it has always been this way and will always be this way. But, if you truly want to be a writer, writing is a compulsion that you have no control over, there is nothing in life that you would rather be doing, then find a small corner of your brain that is not constantly filled with book ideas or characters or self-doubt and insert this thought where it will never get lost – **ODDS ARE ONLY TO BE BEATEN AND IF AT THE END OF YOUR LIFE**

YOU DID NOT BECOME ANOTHER HEMINGWAY, GERTRUDE STEIN, OR STEPHEN KING YOU WILL HAVE LIVED YOUR LIFE THE WAY IT WAS INTENDED – WRITING – and, every so often, ice cream does beat the flame. In many fine dining establishments they serve fried ice cream.

If you are one of those writers who believes a true artist should never make any money from their work and to do so only degrades the true meaning of art I have this to say. You must be rich or married to a rich person as it is extremely difficult to live by eating one's unsold manuscripts even if you put catsup on them – especially e-books as they have zero bulk or fiber.

For those of you trying to make a living as a fiction writer, do not quit your day job, find time to write even if it is only a few minutes a day, write before work, after work, before bed, on the john, riding the bus. Get rid of your TV and write. A page a day in one year is 365 pages. Writing is tough. Life is a bitch and soon we die. Or, to quote someone more profound:

> "In the end everyone is aware of this
> nobody keeps any of what he has
> and life is only a borrowing of bones"

> Pablo Neruda

BE A VOICE NOT AN ECHO

CHAPTER FIVE
AGE OLD QUESTIONS CONCERNING WRITING

When I started writing my mind was a swirling infestation of doubts: How? Why? Am I doing this right? Will people like this? And on and on and on and on. Let's face it, writing is a daunting task that is filled with fear and apprehension. Here is a list of questions that have haunted writers since some person (either an idiot or genius) decided to write a novel.

1) HOW LONG SHOULD A NOVEL BE? A novel can be as long as you want it to be or as short as you want it to be. But, most novels that are published are between 80,000 and 90,000 words. This is purely done for economics – print costs, etc. etc. If you write romances, western, or mysteries, you can query publishers for their word count guidelines. They will even tell you on what pages they want certain things to happen.

For a self-published e-book the word count only affects the charge for a file download which is not a big deal. It might go from 4 cents to a dime. Remember though it is your 4 cents or a dime as it comes out of your royalty.

2) HOW LONG SHOULD A PARAGRAPH BE? As long and as short as you want it or need it to be. I have seen novels with paragraphs pages and pages long and some with so many paragraphs the tab key must be worn out. If a reader likes your book they could really care less how long the paragraphs are.

3) HOW LONG SHOULD A CHAPTER BE? I once received a scathing rejection from an agent informing me that my chapters were too short for a respectable writer. I sent him a copy of a book by a mystery writer that makes close to one hundred million dollars a year whose chapters are normally one or two pages long. I enclosed a letter stating said agent could stick his head where the sun doesn't shine – needless to say I never queried him again. Make your chapters as long or as short as you want.

4) HOW LONG SHOULD A SENTENCE BE? Every writer has their own sentence length. Read ten books and you will see ten different lengths of sentences - short, long, and in between. Write what is comfortable with you. Some people will like it and some will not – so it goes. The object of writing is to please yourself first. If your writing pleases you it will please your readers. The rule of thumb now is to make your sentences different lengths so to engage your reader. I really don't believe this but I suppose it sounds good.

5) WHAT TENSE SHOULD I WRITE IN? Any tense you think is right for the project you are working on and any tense that you are comfortable with. There are books written in every tense and some written in several tenses.

6) IS THERE ANYTHING WRONG WITH WRITING IN FIRST PERSON? First person, second person, 573rd person, it is up to you and only you.

Many people say they really want to write a novel but they do not have the time.

This is my answer. If you write one page a day in one year you will have 365 pages. You might have to give up an hour TV show or some other function you use to waste away your life with but one page a day is nothing. That is the simplest way to write a novel. Plus, once you start there will be days you might, heaven forbid, miss two TV shows and write two pages. If you have the time to go to a bar after work, watch four hours of TV a day, sleep late on Saturday and Sunday morning, you have the time to write a novel. Put your rear end in a chair and write.

There is no one, nobody, no god, no demon, and no nothing that can teach a person how to write. You can be taught how to spell, punctuation, grammar, chew your food with your mouth closed, button your shirt, type, but you cannot be taught how to write. Writers write differently. I can't tell you how you see the sunset. I can't tell you how to feel the wind on your face. I can't tell you what your feet feel like when they touch a beach. You write how you write because **YOU** are **YOU**. Your perspective on the world is yours alone. Does that make any sense? I hope so. Write like **YOU.**

CHAPTER SIX
THE WORD 'JUST' AND A FEW OTHER CHOICE WORDS

You hear it all the time. **DO NOT USE THE WORD 'JUST'- IT IS SLOPPY OR LAZY WRITING.**

Alright, my question is? **WHY NOT USE JUST?** I have seen it used in the majority of best selling books I have read and believe me I have read thousands.

JUST is a word and each and every word has a purpose and a time to be used or not used in a sentence. If it was not meant to be used it would not be a word listed in the dictionary.

JUST is a word that has many meanings – a few are: recently, minimal, a small degree, exactly, absolutely, completely, entirely, perfectly, utterly, wholly, a moment, a second, a short time, not long ago, and, of course as something being fair, open-minded, legally correct, etc. etc. The laws of the land are just, which, if anyone has a working brain knows is a crock of unjust rhetoric.

I just ate. I just finished. I just barely made it. I just don't like them. She just doesn't seem to be able to understand what I am trying to say. Are you just getting home?

You could state: I recently ate. But, how recently did you eat? An hour ago, twenty minutes ago? I just ate means you **JUST** ate.

I just finished. You could state I finished, I finished an hour ago, I finished a few minutes ago, and on and on, or, I just finished – meaning clearly and precisely – I just finished. There is no question of when, there is no question, it is simple and to the point. You could state: I finished. Ok, when did you finish? Or does it matter when you finished? I finished an hour ago. I finished two minutes ago. I finally finished. I **JUST** finished means exactly when you finished, right now.

A few **JUST'S** in your work will not harm anything. Besides, being overly verbose is at times boring or at the worst pretentious. Also, every person who reads, no matter what their educational level, understands the word just. And unless you are **JUST** a professor it is in everyone's day to day language. A few examples where the word **JUST** is difficult to replace: Just go fuck yourself. Just a minute. Just you wait a second (used by parents when trying to control a child.) Just you wait and see. If I have to sit by that person again I think I will just explode.

Don't fret. If the word **JUST** fits, use it, even if other people don't. If you want to use another word use it. If you are fortunate enough for an agent to look at your work or an editor from a press and they want to change it tell them, "Be my guest but make sure you spell my name correctly on the check."

There are many words besides **JUST** considered lazy words by creative writing teachers. Some of these words are: **THEN, VERY, REALLY, IS, THAT, LIKE, SUDDENLY**, to list a few.

DO NOT BE AFRAID TO USE THESE WORDS WHEN THERE IS NO NEED FOR MANY USELESS WORDS TO STATE A SIMPLE THOUGHT, AN IDEA, OR IN CONVERSATION.

When characters talk they do not have a dictionary in their hand nor do they give a damn about proper grammar.

There are also word groups that are frowned on: **TO SEE, TO HEAR, TO THINK, TO WATCH, TO FEEL, CAN, TO DECIDE,** are a few.

AT TIMES ALL OF THESE WILL WORK. THERE IS NO RULE THAT IS CUT IN STONE FOR THEIR USEAGE.

I hear this all the time. If you write **SIT DOWN** you do not have to use down because when you sit it is always down, so write sit and omit down. The same with stand up, when you stand it is always up so write stand. **IF YOU WANT TO WRITE SIT DOWN, LAY DOWN, STAND UP, SIT UP, OR ANY OTHER UNDER-**

STOOD WORDS GO AHEAD AND DO IT. I SEE IT IN NOVELS BOTH WAYS.

Grammar Nazis are constantly reminding people about **THERE, THEIR, THEY'RE.** I will not give the definitions because if I see them one more time I will puke. When a reader is reading a book the majority of the time if there is spelled their they will not even notice it. I have not read many books that have been published that are error free. For some reason the indie market has become inundated with grammar critics that can find the smallest politically incorrect word usage, grammar usage, punctuation mistake in a book and expound on it like it is a mortal sin – all I have to say is these people must be perfect. I have never been able to figure out the perfect bit. I recently read a Steinbeck novel that I suppose deserved a one star review because the word **every** should have been **ever**.

All you perfect people reading this run out and buy all of Steinbeck's books and start reading them – see if you can find it.

TO, TOO, TWO. Even I never mess up two very often.

If you have between $1000 dollars and $2,500 to have your book edited chances are there will still be a mistake in there somewhere. I have had novels read and edited four and five times, not for the usury rates most editors charge, but by well-educated friends who graduated with English degrees and are now teaching and spend most of their time bored out of their minds and sucking up copious amounts of wine. Even with the edits readers still find mistakes. "Dear Mr. Swisher: I enjoyed your 432 page novel but I thought you should know that on page 372 there is a world spelled wrong and on page 475 there should have been their."

A few people say **OFF OF** is a no no. Get off of the sofa - Get off the sofa. She told her son to get off the sofa. She told her son to get off of the sofa. What is the big deal?

The word **DYING** is one word that has always made me wonder what the founders of our modern English language were thinking. Think about this. We are going to **die**. He **died** last week. He thinks he is **dying**. Why is **dying** not spelled **dieing** when **die** and **died** are spelled using d i e? I will **dye** the cloth yellow. I **dyed** the cloth yellow last week. I am **dying** while **dying** the cloth. Is **dying**, meaning to **die**, all about color?

Too many adverbs, not enough adverbs, adverbs show weak writing. If there is such a debate over adverbs why do we even have them as a means of communication? Why didn't some language junky years ago get rid of them all? Why? Because adverbs, like adjectives, and nouns, and pronouns, and any other _____ (fill in the blank with the word of your choice) have a place in writing. If you want to be safe and you think you are using too many adverbs merely cut a few out.

There is a well-established lady author now who will not use quotation marks in conversation. She states they are unnecessary. Example: Mary walked into the bar, looked around, and said, where did all these drunken idiots come from? Do you know what portion of this sentence was conversation? Would you have known if I had left out the question mark that the previous sentence was a question?

At least every other day I get involved with a conversation with people over the use of the word **LIKE** as a lead in for a description. For example: He walked down the street like a frog. When she talked she talked like a tired bullfighter. Many people frown on the word like and say it is weak. A lot of people instead of saying like use **AS IF**. Once again I have read countless books that used the word like. You don't have to use it all the time but don't be afraid to use it.

WRITE DRUNK EDIT SOBER

CHAPTER SEVEN
PUNCTUATION

I have never seen a book review in my 48 years of writing that went something like this: "The punctuation in this book was beautiful. The way the author used commas, colons, periods, dashes, and semi-colons made me both laugh and cry. There was a point in the novel where the Oxford comma use was so profound I was tempted to cut off my hair, buy a red robe, and become a monk. Reading the book I was so enraptured by the punctuation I didn't waste my time trying to follow the story."

There is nothing more debatable or argumentative than the proper way to punctuate. I have stated before that I never use a semi-colon. I don't know if it is because I firmly believe they are useless or I don't like the way they look. If you call me a prejudiced person concerning semi-colons you are right.

There are many authors who punctuate every other word and authors that hardly use any punctuation. Writing fiction has artistic license. You are not writing non-fiction or a text book where, I hate to say, you should use punctuation according to our modern rules, even though these modern rules are based on Latin, Greek, and numerous other obscure languages, which are not modern in my mind, but according to professors are modern enough. "Et tu Brute?" and all that modern stuff.

There was a man a few months ago in one of the writing groups I belong to who lambasted me for my punctuation. He stated in an agitated manner, "It is a sign of ignorance when people do not use proper punctuation and a sign they are lazy." When I informed him many heavy weight reviewing magazines have reviewed my novels and never once mentioned a word about my punctuation he did not reply. I followed with the statement I do not think a lazy person could write a novel unless it took him several hundred years and once again he did not reply. Compare the following sentences:

(1) It was a dark and stormy night and Bill was walking home – he did not know why? But for some reason he had a disturbing premonition – he was going to get killed.

(2) It was a dark and stormy night and Bill was walking home. He did not know why but for some reason he had a disturbing premonition? He was going to get killed.

(3) It was a dark and stormy night and Bill was walking home...he did not know why? But for some reason he had a disturbing premonition (he was going to get killed.)

Question? Did every one of the three statements above have the same meaning?

Did the punctuation in anyway change the meaning?

WHEN PEOPLE READ THEY DO NOT READ PUNCTUATION. For example take this sentence: Why, may I ask, do you not like me? You read this sentence: Why may I ask do you not like me? You did not read it – Why comma may I ask comma do you not like me question mark.

Read this sentence several times. Now that Melinda was gone Bill could not drive the thought of her out of his mind even though he tried with every ounce of willpower and mental resolve he could muster in his sadly depressed and overburdened state.

WHEN PEOPLE READ THEY PUT BREAKS OR PAUSES IN WHAT THEY READ THAT ARE INDIVIDUAL TO THEM. THESE PATTERNS ARE SET BY THE WAY THEY SPEAK AND NOT BY WHAT FORM OR THE PLACEMENT OF THE PUNCTUATION THAT IS USED.

I was reading the other day where a famous author, now dead of course, stated that the explanation mark was a sign of bad writing. Help!! I take it this author, who will remain unnamed, had nothing to do in his life but talk about exclamation points and drink. If you think exclamation points are unnecessary dribble and do not belong in a properly written work of fiction don't use them. If you think this dead author is full of hot air go ahead and use them to your hearts content. What easier way to show alarm, excitement, dread, fear, etc. etc. than with an exclamation point. If you are a real radical use two or three in a row – now that is really living on the edge.

A novel of mine was slammed by a Grammar Nazi for using 's after the name Jones. Example: Jones's. The Grammar Nazi went into fits that I wrote Jones's all the way through the manuscript. Ladies and gentlemen, boys and girls, you can write Jones' or Jones's – they are both correct. The main thing is whatever you do, do it consistently throughout the manuscript. For the Grammar Nazi that was so offended I take it you never read **Bridget Jones's Diary** by Helen Fielding – sold a zillion copies and was made into a movie.

I really think some bored English teacher was sitting around one day and decided to make up punctuation marks so he or she could give more students failing grades. Either that or they thought diagramming sentences would save the world. Here are a few other punctuation marks people seem to have mini-heart attacks over.

DOTS: ... means a pause, delay, whatever you want to call it. Grammar Nazis say to only use three dots, anything over three dots is a major sin. How about? .... means a long pause and more dots .... a longer pause.

One day a bored out of their mind English teacher or grammar Nazi was sitting around and decided they would write a paper about the two **DASHES** (en dash and em dash) and how important they are to the true meaning and depth of a story. Without the proper use of a dash all thought, all depth, all the intrinsic and important parts of a book, a poem, or a short story is ruined. Please? A dash is a dash. Does this dash – mean more to you than this dash - ? And please don't tell me either one of these dashes has anything to do with storytelling or meaning.

A hyphen is a hyphen and not even a distant cousin to either of the two dashes.

I use a lot of dashes. I use dashes instead of semi-colons because I dislike semi-colons. It is a personal thing. But to make Grammar Nazis have hot flashes I seldom use em dashes. I simply don't like the way the em-dash looks. If you want to give me an F it is ok – I can live with it. What I am saying is dashes work for anything you want them to – they are a pause like a comma. They can also be used in place of colons if you want to list things. They can replace semi-colons. The person reading the story or novel, unless they are a Grammar Nazi would care less. **IT IS THE STORY THEY ARE INTERESTED IN. (Writing this book I have used both dashes. Have you noticed?)**

The world is besieged with wars, starvation, inequality, racism, and a changing climate. But all of these plights pale to Grammar Nazi's arguments whether the **OXFORD COMMA,** more properly named the Serial Comma, (the final comma used in a list of things), should be used or not used. My solution to the problem is why not get rid of all commas and use a series of periods or dashes for all pauses, lists, or anything else you wanted. Example using the Oxford comma: We sell guns, chewing gum, and health food products. Not using the Oxford comma: We sell guns, chewing gum and health food products. Here is my solution: We sell guns – chewing gum – and health food products. We sell guns...chewing gum...and health food products.

BRACKETS have always confused me. I know they are used within a text to set apart other text, but why set apart other text when you can merely write another sentence. I do know I like the way they look and when I use them for some reason they give me a fleeting sense of being intelligent, which I know is a lie, because if I was intelligent I would not be a writer of fiction (I would write non-fiction.)

When it gets down to the basics when writing fiction **PUNCTUATE THE WAY YOU WANT.** If you want to use dashes instead of semi colons be my guest. If you want to use five dots instead of three go ahead. If you like exclamation marks use them. If you don't like exclamation marks don't use them. If you don't want to use a colon when you are about to run off a list don't worry about it. Remember, with fiction, you have artistic license, but as with most everything in life don't go overboard.

CHAPTER EIGHT
SPELLING

I read and read and read and read and read a manuscript looking diligently for spelling errors. My wife reads and reads over the same manuscript looking for spelling errors. I spell check the manuscript a minimum of twenty times. An editor, normally a friend, reads and reads over the manuscript. After all of this there has only been one time in all of my published 24 novels a reader has not found a spelling error.

I worked on a historical novel for close to two years, placed it with a small publisher, and after correcting the galleys the publisher printed the novel from the uncorrected galleys. Go figure. I was and still am sick about it – the worst thing is the book is still in print.

Rule of thumb: **A FEW SPELLING ERRORS WILL BE OVERLOOKED BY A READER BUT TOO MANY SPELLING ERRORS AND YOUR NOVEL, NO MATTER HOW GOOD, HOW EPIC, HOW WONDERFUL IN CONTENT AND SCOPE, AND DEPTH OF CHARACTERS, WILL BE DEAD IN THE WATER. I REPEAT – DEAD IN THE WATER.**

Read your work until you cannot take it anymore, set it aside for a week, a month, and then read it again. A writer, no matter how careful, reads over words they have written, even at times reading in a word that they have omitted. It has been proven we really only form words in our mind by a few of the first letters and the last.

Some people say to reread your manuscript from the back forward. Read each page from bottom to top. Whatever way you like to check over your work all I can really say is it is drudgery and good luck. There is no easy way or shortcut.

DON'T QUIT YOUR DAY JOB

CHAPTER NINE
THE MYTH OF SHOW DON'T TELL

When one is in front of a group of people do they show a story or do they tell a story? "Ladies and gentlemen, tonight we have the esteemed writer Mr. Robert K. Swisher Jr. and he is going to **SHOW** us a story."

At which time I signal my camera crew, a screen drops down, and they proceed to show a portion of my book.

Show don't tell has been beaten into writer's brains so often most writer's skulls have to have a flat side from the repeated blows. "Show don't tell is a technique to enable the reader to experience the story through action, words, thoughts, senses, and feelings rather than the author's exposition..." Well, I am not the first to say this, but, to show all the time and not tell is impossible and if you did show all the time a novel that should be 100,000 words would be 200,000 words – 100,000 of them wasted showing words. Don't worry about showing and not telling, write your story, you will know if you went overboard or an editor will tell you. As usual, there are bestselling books that show and there are bestselling books that tell. I bet if you asked the normal reader what show don't tell is they would wonder what the hell you are talking about.

Nothing to do about show don't tell but I was reading an online writing blog the other day and the person spent three paragraphs explaining that contractions should never be used while writing, which means: can't, don't, won't, isn't, shouldn't, ain't, and on and on are words that make one a weak writer. Unless you are writing in 16th century proper English I suppose this would hold true but for modern writing, especially conversation, it makes no sense what so ever to me.

CHAPTER TEN
WRITE WHAT YOU KNOW

From the novice writer to the seasoned veteran you hear over and over again **WRITE WHAT YOU KNOW.** This is a statement that has always bewildered me. I get bewildered easily but that is beside the point.

When I was teaching my anti-establishment writing class there would come a day when without notice or fanfare I would ask the class. "What is one thing you understand about what you should write?"

Most everyone would reply with a knowing smile on their face. "Write what you know."

I would pick a student and have them come to the front of the class, hand them a piece of chalk, and say, "Ok, write something you do not know on the chalk board."

They would ponder for a few moments and say, "I can't write what I don't know."

"Correct," I would say. "You can only write what you know. If you don't know it you can't write it."

No matter if you write science fiction, westerns, romances, whatever, you know about the idea or you could not write the story. Your knowledge is your brain - your dreams, your fantasies. You do not have to go to the beach to know what the ocean sounds like. You do not have to visit the moon to know what the surface of the moon is like. You do not have to have experienced a broken heart to know what a broken heart feels like. **YOU CAN ONLY WRITE WHAT YOU KNOW.** If not books would be easy to write. They would be nothing but blank pages. Think about it.

WRITING IS A JOURNEY NOT AN EVENT

CHAPTER ELEVEN
MERELY FOR FUN

During my failed college career I had a writing professor who went into great detail about what the underlying meaning was to what an author actually wrote. If the author wrote, "I want to hold your hand." The professor said what the author really meant was that he was tortured by the demons of his insane mother and he wanted to lick the elbows of every woman with blond hair between the ages of 17 and 22 years old.

If an author wrote the sky was azure blue he really meant the state of the economy in Brazil was having a negative impact on his writing and he had been fantasizing about starting a revolution but all he could afford were two cases of BB guns.

Truthfully, the majority of the time, I don't think a writer really knows where the words are coming from and what he writes he really means. The sky was blue means the sky was blue. He was sick means he was sick. But I suppose when you are teaching there has to be some deep and dark inner meaning to about everything.

I asked my creative writing professor if the author intended to say something else why didn't he just say it. The professor looked at me like only an idiot would ask such a question. The question could also be the reason I got a D- for the semester.

CHAPTER TWELVE
ONCE AGAIN IN CASE YOU HAVE FORGOTTEN – YOU CANNOT TEACH HOW TO WRITE FICTION

I mentioned this earlier in the book that fiction writing cannot be taught. You can be taught the alphabet, how to spell, how to punctuate for whatever way is the norm of the day, what a verb is, a noun, a pronoun, an adverb, all the clauses, and on and on. But you cannot be taught how to take all of these parts and make them into a book. Writing fiction is a calling – an instinct – something inside of you that wants to come out in a manner that is not hindered by rules and definitions. Let it come out the way it is intended – not governed by the definitions of others.

The majority of people have a job that they hate, not all, but most. I have never met a writer that is truly content unless they are writing – if there is such a thing as a contented writer. Writing is more of a blissful agony. But, even so, a writer would not change his life to be anything else.

There are millions of books explaining how to write a novel – half of these are written by writers who think the way they write a novel is the way every writer in the world should write a novel. These books cover character development, pacing, structure, how to sit on the toilet, and on and on. Some people outline a book before they begin writing. Some people blast through a first draft and could care less about anything but getting the idea out. I know a writer that writes a chapter at a time and corrects everything as he goes. I get an idea, start writing, and the story goes where it wants to go. Professors call this stream of consciousness. I call it I have no idea what the hell is going on. I know writers that write long hand, some use a computer, some still have typewriters, some dictate, and some have people write for them. **WHAT EVER WAY YOU LIKE TO WRITE DO IT. IF YOU LIKE AN IDEA WRITE IT. IF YOU WRITE NAKED SITTING IN FRONT OF A MIRROR WHILE EATING SPAGHETTI HAVE FUN.**

What is muse if it is not your own?

DON'T THINK JUST WRITE

CHAPTER THIRTEEN
THE SECRETS OF WRITING

There are no secrets to writing. Writing is work. If you don't know how to work you can't be a writer. If you are waiting for inspiration to be a writer you might wait a long time, writing is 1% inspiration and the rest exasperation. But, here are a few tips that **MIGHT** help your writing addiction.

1) Put your butt in the chair and write
2) Set aside a certain time each day and keep at it
3) When you don't feel like writing – write anyway
4) Put your butt in the chair and write
5) There is no need to set a word limit for each day – each day will be different
6) Getting up from your chair and moving around helps
7) If you are writing for the market research the market
8) Put your butt in the chair and write
9) Don't make up excuses
10) Put your butt in the chair and write
11) Believe in your writing – do not compare yourself to others
12) Put your butt in the chair and write

13) Don't give up – there are no guarantees in writing or life

14) Good luck, good destiny, good whatever you want to call it

I wrote one novel in a closet while my wife and baby slept. I wrote one novel in a garage warmed by a kerosene heater. I wrote one novel when we were so broke I set the computer on a cardboard box. I wrote a novel in Vietnam that on the day I was to fly back to the world I threw away. There is always time to write if you really want to.

CHAPTER FOURTEEN
EDITORS

Writers have an obsession with editors - especially the indie writers. There are copy editors, content editors, line by line editors, beta readers, and somewhere in the vast universe of editors I bet there is an editor for blank pages. In my humble opinion the majority of editors are overpriced but since writers will pay their fees there is not much that can be done about it. My editor is a complete editor and reasonably priced. My wife reads and corrects my books and I get one of two comments: "It's good or it sucks."

Let me set something straight: **THERE ARE NO TWO EDITORS THAT WILL EDIT A BOOK THE SAME WAY.** I will say this again: **THERE ARE NO TWO EDITORS THAT WILL EDIT A BOOK THE SAME WAY.** Find an editor you like and stick with them. Also look around. $2,000 to edit a novel is ridiculous. There are many editors who work for reasonable rates – but be careful and it is a good rule of thumb to never use an editor that does not come with references from people you know. And, for your information, if an agent says they like your book but it should be sent to a book doctor who they recommend and for a fee, **DON'T DO IT!!** It is a scam and the agent and book doctor will split the money.

Years ago I had a friend who had written several best-selling novels. We started talking about editors. He said to me, "Listen Bob, editors are like a Jew, a Catholic, a Baptist, and a Born Again Christian trying to explain to each other what God truly is."

He also had another bit of wisdom. "You know you are a writer when you forget how many submissions you have out while writing another book.

ROUGH DRAFTS ARE JUST THAT - ROUGH DRAFTS

CHAPTER FIFTEEN
COPYRIGHT

A fear for many writers is copyright. **DO NOT WORRY ABOUT COPYRIGHT!!** I will holler again - **DO NOT WORRY ABOUT COPYRIGHT!!** I hate to say this but unless you are a world famous writer nobody wants to steal your blood soaked and profound words and even if they did there is really not much they can do with them. Your novel, poem, short story, novella, memoir, or biography, anything you have written is copyrighted automatically for your life and 70 years.

If you are paranoid, put a hard copy of your work in an envelope and mail it to yourself and do not open it. If any question would ever arise that you are the creator of said work the post office has stamped dates all over the package for proof. If you do not want to mail it in fear the post office will lose your manuscript take the sealed envelope to the post office, have them stamp the dates on the seams, pay the postage and get it marked as mailed, and take it home. Proof positive you are the author. That's it. It is not complicated. Do not fret.

If you have self published a book on Amazon or any other site and you see one of your books on an illegal site once again do not fret. Pirated e-books on illegal sites do not generate many sales – if anything it gives you some free promotion and the satisfaction your work is worth stealing.

If you are world famous and someone in China illegally prints one of your books and sells a million copies there is not much you can do about it.

Here is a dirty little secret about the publishing industry. If you are ever lucky and have a best seller get ready for the onslaught of law suits stating you plagiarized some of their material. Most of these are settled out of court because it is cheaper. If you want an extreme example of plagiarism law suits read the gory lawsuit ridden history of **ROOTS** by Alex Haley.

CHAPTER SIXTEEN
ROYALTIES BOTH TRADITIONAL AND SELF PUBLISHED AND A FEW COMMENTS ON BOOK PROMOTION

Humans constantly worry about how much money we will get paid. We have to unless you are a member of a remote tribe of subsistence hunter gatherers. In our society it takes money to be born, live, and then die, which is the main reason we are stressed out most of the time, but it keeps the government happy and laughing at us because the majority of us believe we enjoy freedom. If working 40 to 60 hours a week, or two jobs, and getting a few holidays off a year is freedom I wonder what not having freedom is.

The normal first novel published by a trade publisher, even the big boys, seldom sells more than a few thousand copies. This does not mean your book will not sell 1,487,372 copies and make you so famous you will buy a castle in the UK, an island that is so remote it is not on the map, will be given 137 honoree degrees from universities around the world, and asked your opinion on every subject that you really know nothing about. But, to be realistic, if a book sells 10,000 copies it is a great sale. So, let's break down the money. Let's say you signed a contract for 10% of the royalties. The normal contract is 12% graduated by increments of sales but for this example I will use 10% mainly because my math skills are terrible. Let's say your book is listed for $16.00. This means the book store will get the book for between 55% and 40% off the cover price. I will use 50%. The book store gets the book for $8.00. 10% of $8.00 is 80 cents. You will receive 80 cents for the sale. If you were lucky and the book sold 10,000 copies you would receive $8,000. Not bad, if you were published by a name house that takes agented work only you would owe your agent 15% of the $8000. Many agents now charge 20%. Then you owe self-employment taxes and have the great fortune of having to file quarterly. Also, the agent receives the money from the publisher and then pays you. There are a few authors who receive a percentage of the list price – normally the ones who have made so much money royalties really have little meaning anymore – they are making fortunes on speaking fees. Under the modern contract you are also expected to generate much of your own publicity with your own dime. That is unless you are an actor or actress informing the world how many people you have slept with or how many past lives you can remember. Most book tours now are paid for by the author after they hire a book publicist, who has all the connections, which costs from $5,000 to $20,000 a month. A small publisher might set up book signings for you at book stores where you have to get there on your own dime. Selling ten books at each book store on a six state book tour does not pay for the gas, let alone the fast food, but they are great fun and you get to meet people and see different parts of the country.

One thing a publisher will do is send as many review copies as they can to reviewers before the book release date. This costs you nothing, but if you want copies to try and generate your own reviews you will have to buy the book at normally 50% of cover – you will not receive royalties from copies you purchase. Both good and bad reviews will get you sales.

There is a monster in the book industry called returns or remainders. For an example: A publisher prints 2,000 copies of your novel and sends them out to book stores. Only 1,000 sell at full price, the others are then remaindered and sold at a discount, normally 2 to 4 dollars. Figure your royalty on those – two cents to a dime.

There are also returns. 2,000 copies of your novel sells, 500 are returned. Guess who gets a smaller check? If you received a small advance, let's say $2,500. And your royalty came to $2,000. You owe the publisher $500. Damn, you say, the cost of fame. If you have a decent agent he will have had you sign a multi-book contract and you will not have to worry about paying them as they will publish another book.

All the paperback books you see at flea markets without covers are books that were stolen and somehow made it back to the public. If a chain book store receives 5,000 paperbacks and only sells 2,000 the other 3,000 have their covers ripped off and are tossed in the garbage – the publisher does not even want them back and sorry – no royalty.

Merely for a comparison, a self-published e-book through Nook, Amazon, or the other sites. I mean a book you did yourself, not through one of the many crooked e-book self publishers (these are covered in another chapter) A book that you list for $3.99 will make more money per copy than a traditional publisher. Their normal royalty rate on an e-book is 70%.

If you self publish a print on demand paper copy of a book it is unlikely you will be able get them into traditional brick and mortar book stores as the printer will not accept returns. An exception to the return policy is Ingram Sparks a division of Lightening Source print on demand publisher – they take returns, but it is still difficult to get into a brick and mortar book store although not impossible - some more on this later in the chapter. You will be able to put your paper copy in local libraries, gift shops, and use them for book signings you can independently set up – flea markets, farmers markets, author writing clubs, grocery stores, and places where you can set up a booth. Don't forget promo in local art magazines.

Getting self-published books into Barnes and Noble Book Stores is hard but not impossible. They now have a small press department you can mail two copies of your book to and they will consider carrying it. The book does have to be returnable. Your local Barnes and Noble will do signings for your book - once again it must be returnable.

Independent book stores, even though they call themselves independent, are also hard to get your books into unless they are returnable. They are more open to local authors but many of them have started small press and indie book consignment deals. Myself I think consignment deals are a crock of _____ (insert any word you like) and I will not do them or recommend others to. The book store will say for a filing fee of from $25.00 to $75.00 to pay for the time it takes to catalog your books you can place 3 to 6 copies in their store for a 60/40 split: 60% for the author and 40% for the store means you will make a few dollars a book if you are lucky which means if they sell 6 books you make $12.00 for giving them $25.00. In the modern world it takes a few seconds to get on the computer and enter a new title onto the inventory sheet. Plus, since to get in the store the book has to be returnable all a book store has to do is buy the books for 50% off cover and if they don't sell send them back and get their money back.

Another thing independent book stores are doing is charging fees for small presses and indie authors to hold book signings or readings. The fees range from $100 to more. That's big of them as setting up a table in the corner by the entrance to the bathroom really takes a lot of time and effort.

One thing you must always do on a self-published or small press book is have your name and title of the book on the spine or a bookstore will not even consider your book as books are placed on shelves spine out. This is not true for the new Amazon brick and mortar stores – the books are placed with the cover facing out.

A small press recently published a novel of mine. We decided because of the nature of the book we would promote the print version to independent book stores more than online promotion for the e-book. We designed a release with a brief description, several reviews, what made the book unique, details about book store rate, returns, page length, and a picture of the cover. There has been a response rate on an average of one reply for every twenty proposals. The majority of independent bookstores do not even take the twenty seconds to hit reply and type in **NO THANK YOU**.

Small presses and indie authors can now submit their books to Midwest Book Review and the indie division of Publishers Weekly - most major reviewing organizations will still not review print on demand books (the snob effect is still doing well in the publishing industry.)

With a self-published book you completely toot your own horn. Toot loud and often, research the indie sites that sell books. The general rule of thumb is that you need a blog, an author page, a web site, and get on as many social media sites that you can. If you want to do this, but don't want to waste the time and spend your time writing you can hire people to do it for you. But, there are many self-published writers that avoid social media and do fine marketing through indie promotion sites. Through my own endeavors I have found most writing groups online are mainly composed of other authors trying to sell their books. There are many writing groups that their purpose is for questions, help, and a shoulder to cry on when needed.

I have done reasonably well selling my self-published books on indie-book sales sites. There are many indie promotion sites out there – some are free, some are $10.00, some are $50.00, some are close to $1,000. There are complete lists of reviewing sites on the web. I use close to thirty of them. Research your sites carefully, ask questions, and be careful, the indie world is beginning to get infested with crooks and malicious trolls much like the traditional publishing industry has been for years. The anonymity of the internet makes it possible for cowards and crooks to roam freely.

NEVER FORGET YOUR DREAM

CHAPTER SEVENTEEN
QUERY LETTER, SYNOPSIS, AND ALL THAT OTHER GUT WRENCHING STUFF

You have written your book, now it gets down to the fun stuff. If you are trying to get published by a traditional publisher, an e-book publisher, a small press, or seeking an agent, you will have to write a query letter and a synopsis of your masterpiece. **BUT**, even the mention of the word query letter or synopsis sends most authors into a fit of paranoia and feeling like they are falling into a bottomless hole.

At my last count there are approximately two billion books, articles, posts on the internet, and advice columns on how to correctly write a query letter and a synopsis.

Basically, when it gets down to the twixt of the matter, you are trying to kiss the posterior of either an agent or a publisher, and since most publishers only read material submitted by agents the majority of agent's posteriors get kissed a lot.

Do not worry yourself to death as you start the dreaded process of writing a query letter or a synopsis. You can throw-up a few times as it may help purge your body and mind and get you closer to your center but worry does no good. If you find it impossible to write a query letter, thanks to the wonders of the modern world, there are people that for a small fee will write one for you. I have found some for as little as $50.00. If you cannot afford the small fee you are stuck writing your own – sorry, it's a rough life.

Here is the bottom line. There is no one way to write a query letter or a synopsis. There is no deep dark hidden secret that has been passed down from generation to generation by an order of writing monks who live somewhere in the sewers of New York City that will guarantee if you follow their way to write a query letter or synopsis all the publishers or agents in the world will fight over who gets to kiss your posterior and publish your masterpiece.

LISTEN TO ME: Agents or publishers will state in their guidelines **EXACTLY** what they want in their query letter or synopsis down to the **EXACT LENGTH** they wish it to be and what they want it to **EXACTLY** cover and to whom they **EXACTLY** want it mailed or e-mailed to. Since you are doing your best to kiss their posterior do what they **EXACTLY** say. Let me say this again: **DO EXACTLY WHAT THEY STIPULATE IN THEIR GUIDELINES.**

And yes they are both hard to write but I have to this day found nothing that is easy to write. If writing is easy for you please e-mail me and tell me your secret and maybe we can collaborate on a book that I promise the majority of writers who find writing difficult and gut wrenching will buy.

Here are a few tips: If the agent or publisher you are approaching is one of the few that only accept paper queries use good paper and have a good letterhead. And, on an e-mail query do not forget it is still a query and set it up as such – a true business proposal in letter format. Dear the person's name not Dear Editor.

Here is a dirty little secret about submissions - no, it does not involve ropes, chains, handcuffs, or things that vibrate. When you submit to publishers or agents they want to be notified if you are submitting only to them or to multiple agencies. I always sent my queries out five to ten at a time, never mentioned I was submitting to others, and never got into a wreck by two people wanting to read the material at the same time – normally there were many submissions I didn't get a reply from anyway. As soon as I received a rejection I mailed out another query.

One reason I never feel bad about sending off multiple submission is the fact that most agents, when they submit proposals to publishers, submit more than one book at a time.

Good luck with your queries and synopsis. Remember, writing them will not kill you, they will only make you wish you werc dead.

CHAPTER EIGHTEEN
CONTRACTS

I have signed a few lousy contracts in my day and my advice comes from several painful experiences.

A normal book contract takes three attorneys to figure out. But since the average writer cannot afford an attorney to go over the contract I am going to inform you about a few important things you should look out for. A publisher tries their best to get the best deal they can get for themselves – the best deal being how little they can pay you. Don't think they want to publish your book because they think you are a nice person and you need a break in this big bad world. **THEY WANT TO PUBLISH YOUR BOOK BECAUSE THEY THINK THEY CAN MAKE SOME MONEY.** They will not publish a book that they think will not make money. Years ago most presses kept a mid-list group of writers and published small runs of their work to keep them alive and the fact they enjoyed their writing. No more, corporations own publishing houses now, not readers and lovers of books, and corporations only think about one thing – the thing being the bottom line. This is one reason, not to slam many writers, but this is one reason most of the books that are published now have little to do with literature. The presses print what sells. I hate this statement but it is how it is. If you write literary fiction a tough business became tougher – you can thank the small and literary presses for keeping some form of literature alive – without them the majority of published books would not stimulate the brain of an ant – sorry – this is how I feel.

Make sure that any contract you sign has a stipulation that you can get the rights back to your books – this may mean if they don't sell, if the publisher does nothing with them, there are many reasons just make sure you can get your book rights back. You might state after three years you have an option to take your rights back. I have several old novels now that are still in print, sitting in limbo, that I am trying to get the rights back as I know I could generate at least a small amount of interest as indie e-books. At the present rate it will take me until I am 106 years old.

Try not to sign a contract where the publisher wants right of first refusal. This means they want the first look at the next book you write. You don't know your first book might do so well another publisher would offer you a better deal on the second. This is a difficult clause to get rid of but it is worth a try.

Stipulate a payment schedule when you will get paid, will it be every six months, every three months, once a year. Make sure it is clear and make sure it is on time. There is also a clause at times that states if the publisher only owes you $25.00 dollars or so they will not pay you until the next time. Get rid of this. If they owe they owe. If they do not pay in time demand your rights back as to the stipulation in your contract.

Try to get a royalty step up plan. For example: You get 10% for the first 2,500 copies sold, 12% from 2,500 copies to 10,000 copies sold, and 15% for all copies sold over 10,000.

There are all types of rights that come with a publishing deal. Serial rights, movie rights, reprint rights, book club rights, paperback rights, world rights, and on and on. Most of these are split 50/50 with the publisher. If you self publish they belong to you. If an e-book publisher wants to split rights I would do no less than 70/30 for the writer. Also with an e-book publisher make sure you have a stipulation when you can get the e-book rights back – is it by written consent, two years, breach of contract, make it clear and precise. And how often will you get paid? **HAVE EVERYTHING SPELLED OUT IN WRITING.** If an e-book company wants to do your book and you agree make sure you keep the rights for a traditional printed book.

The thing about an e-book publisher is the fact it is relatively inexpensive to create an e-book. If they do not have an extensive following you might as well do it by yourself.

Even though there are many crooks in the business the majority of publishers are as honest as a true capitalist can be. If a publisher is interested in your book they will normally agree to a few of the things you want changed in your contract. Signing a contract is like buying a car, negotiate and do not be afraid to state what you think is fair, and stick to your guns.

There Are a Lot of Words in Both a Short Story and a Novel

CHAPTER NINETEEN
TO SELF PUBLISH OR NOT AND FREE-BOOKS

A question many writers are torn by is to self-publish or try the traditional path? I would always try the traditional path first. Send out queries, try to get an agent, after a year or two with no luck there is always the indie world.

IF YOU DECIDE TO SELF PUBLISH DO NOT, DO NOT, DO NOT, GO WITH ANY COMPANY THAT WILL CHARGE YOU TO DO ALL THE WORK AND SAY THEY WILL HELP PROMOTE YOUR BOOK. THEY ARE CROOKS. There are many of these companies out there. There is an internet site called **WRITERS BEWARE.** You can contact them and they will research any press for you and they do have a list of presses to stay away from.

There is a ploy by many presses that they will cover the price of publishing your book but you have to buy so many copies before the release - normally at 40 percent below cover price which is less than a bookstore would get them for. If you question why you have to buy your own book before release the publisher will say they want to make sure their authors will work to sell the book. Bullshit. Your purchase will pay all the set up fees plus a small profit to the press and you do not get royalties from books you purchase. Stay away from these presses. A true publisher is willing to risk losing money on your book to make money. And a true publisher will sell you as many of your books you like for bookstore rates although you do not receive royalties on books you purchase.

You have heard about a few now famous writers that got their start by self-publishing their work. There are not many but there are a few. With the advent of Amazon, Nook, Kobo, and other companies self-publishing is not as frowned on as it once was. You can also rest assured Amazon, Nook, Kobo and other sites are not crooks. If you can design your own cover, convert your files into mobi and e-pub, and follow simple uploading instructions then presto your book is on the market as an e-book or a print on demand trade paper. If you don't have the ability covers and file conversion is not expensive and there are many people out there who are honest and do good work. Both Smashwords and CreateSpace have a list of reputable people who specialize in conversion files and covers.

Once your book is live you can now spend hours begging for reviews, doing review swaps, or what ever else you can think of for people to read your book and leave a review. Then with enough good reviews you can start trying to get your book onto online reading promotion sites who will sell your book.

There are many debates as to what price one should price their indie e-book. Some say $2.99, some $3.99, and on and on. What difference does it make if you can only put your book up for sale through promotion sites if it is reduced to 99 cents or $1.99? Myself I feel an indie e-book should be listed for $4.99. For paper books you should try to set your price lower than the norm to increase your chances for sales. A traditional publishing company when they release a novel as both e-book and paper normally lists their e-books from between $7.95 and $14.95 which is ridiculous as they pay no more to have an e-book produced than you do – but so it goes.

When it comes to indie audio books I have not made up my mind if they are worth the expense or not? If you have deep pockets you can make your book an e-book, paper, and audio. I would wait for two or three books that were successful and then do an audio book on the fourth or fifth book.

Author's wonder if they should place their e-books on all the e-book sites or only Amazon. I have had good luck with Amazon, fair with the others, but when I do want to reach many sites I use Draft-2-Digctal for distribution (they will put your e-book on all the sites that mean something and they pay regularly.) It is all up to you, what works for some does not work for others.

Several years ago some Einstein had the idea that if they started giving their books away for free they would get higher rankings on Amazon and Nook. I am opposed to free-books. If people are giving away books for free where is the incentive to buy a book? If I had a car lot and gave my cars away would you go next door and buy a car from another dealer? If I had a bar and gave beer away would you go to another bar and buy beer? Some writers have informed me by giving away a book in a series it leads to sales for other books. In my experience this is only partially true. If I have given away 9,000 books how many people will buy another book when all they have to do is get another free book? Would those same 9,000 have purchased the book for 99 cents or would they have ignored the book and picked up a free-book? I have also been told free books will lead to more reviews. Statistics show that less than 40 percent of free books get read and less than 10% of people leave a review. When gas is free, along with food, and clothes, I do not have to pay taxes, beer is free, and on and on, I will give away free books. I think in many ways free books have cut the throat of indie authors. I do give away free books to reviewers.

For self-publishers who think they have a good enough book to have a chance of getting into book stores you

should produce one book with CreateSpace but do not use expanded distribution. CreateSpace does not take returns, so bookstores will not carry their books, but you can purchase books for events you supply the inventory for. Set up another copy of the same book with Ingram Spark – there is a $49.00 fee and their formatting is slightly different for the cover due to paper differences. Ingram Spark will take returns and give you a chance at getting into book stores.
NOTE: CreateSpace books are cheaper for you to buy. You also will need an ISBN, which can be used for both Ingram and CreateSpace as it is the same book. You can purchase your ISBNs through Bowkers. You should also get a Library of Congress Number which is free and could result in library sales. I recommend setting up your own small press if you go this route which is not difficult.

CHAPTER TWENTY
BOOK REVIEWS AND TROLLS

Reviews are necessary for the success of any traditionally published or indied book. For the book published by a traditional publisher review copies are sent out before release (normally four months in advance) any good reviews are then put on the jacket. It has been recently proven that reviews by other authors get more people to buy the book than reviews by big name reviewers.

For the indie e-book publisher gathering reviews is a different monster. You can get reviews from a list of people who have read other books of yours, listing on reviewing sites (which there are hundreds) swapping reviews with other authors, or any other plan you can dream up. There is a long list on the internet of bloggers that review indie books. Try everything and everything in your power to garner reviews – some ideas will work some will not. Do not pay for reviews. It helps if at the end of your book you put a statement: **IF YOU ENJOYED THIS BOOK WOULD YOU PLEASE POST A REVIEW ON YOUR FAVORITE REVIEWING SITE** and leave your author page, webpage, or e-mail so a reader may contact you.

I have stated this before but The Midwest Book Review and the indie division of Publishers Weekly main objective is reviewing small presses, university presses, and self-published books. Look up their guidelines. The best time for indies and small publishers to try for mainstream reviews is during the off seasons when the big publishers are taking a breather.

The worst thing about the reviewing process is that it has created a certain beast called a **TROLL**. A troll is a person who attacks a book and leaves a 1 star review normally after only reading a few pages. There are troll groups that will attack an author and leave many 1 star reviews. Why they do this is anyone's guess: they like to hurt people, they have a book in the same category and are trying to get rid of the competition, they are merely jerks, or their mommy took their allowance away. You cannot escape them and you will get trolled. The best thing to do is do nothing. Let them crawl back into their hole and snicker over their childish actions. On the brighter side many people will read a book because of a bad review just to see if the person who left the review really knows what they are talking about or are just being spiteful. I imagine this book will get hundreds of 1 star reviews from Grammar Nazis.

WRITING IS AN ENJOYABLE AGONY

CHAPTER TWENTY ONE
RANDOM QUESTIONS

Some of the following questions were covered in the text but it does not hurt to repeat a few of them. I for one can say my short term memory is not the best.

1) Does a writer need a blog?

Some writers have done well with a blog and some have not. But fundamentally it can help you more than not. One thing I have noticed is writers that break up their blogging by talking about other subjects besides their books tend to generate better results. When it comes to websites I don't see a great deal of difference between a Facebook Author Page and a website - although I do have both and wonder at times why.

2) How many social media sites should I belong to?

Only the number you can manage and still have time to write. If you have money you can hire someone to manage your social media sites.

3) Is a paid Kirkus Review worth the money?

I would never pay for a review but there have been books that have gone over the top with a paid Kirkus Review. If you have an extra $400 and want to take a chance it will be a good review go for it.

4) Are there really any set in stone rules for writing fiction?

Beyond spelling correctly the answer is no.

5) Can a book be written in several tenses?

Yes

6) Do I have to use proper punctuation while writing fiction?

There is poetic license just don't let it get out of hand.

7) Is it ok to submit work to more than one agent or publisher at a time?

I always did. My number was ten when one submitted in an envelope. Now with most submissions being by e-mail send out as many as you want. Most will not respond anyway. If you want to say it is not a simultaneous submission that is up to you. **ONE THING THAT IS IMPORTANT FOR YOUR SUBMISSION IS FOLLOW THE GUIDELINES TO THE T.** Agents and publishers are normally pompous and unforgiving. Your work will be tossed without even a look. Most of the time the main agent or publisher does not read submissions – they have an assistant looking for keywords. A list of agents can be found on the internet by category. I think it is a better list than the print version of Writer's Market. There are also sites you can check the credibility of an agent.

8) What is the advised length for a novel?

There is no set length. Some novels take 80,000 words - some 200,000 words. The novel will tell you when enough is enough. When it comes to short stories for magazines the magazine will tell you their word count and there are some book imprints that in their guidelines will also state how many words they are looking for. If a romance imprint states they are interested in novels between 65,000 words and 80,000 don't send them a novel with 135,000 words.

9) How do I write a query letter?

There are 2,468,193 thousand books and articles on how to write a query letter. My advice is to make it short and to the point and think you are writing the back cover blurb for your book.

10) How do I write a synopsis?

There are 3,482,735 thousand books and articles on how to write a synopsis. I drink two bourbons on the rocks, look at my computer screen for several hours, start typing, delete, start typing, delete, drink another bourbon, start typing, delete, and normally within a week or two I have a synopsis and a terrible headache. The best way I have found to write a synopsis is have a friend read your novel and write one for you. Every writer dreads writing a synopsis. It is one of those **"PERILS OF THE TRADE"** deals every profession has.

11) I never have enough time to write what can I do?

If you eat, sleep, watch TV, go to the movies, work, walk, play, talk, go to a bar, dance on the weekend, read in bed, or anything else that deals with being alive you have time to write. One page a day in a year is 365 pages. I wrote my first book in a closet in a one room apartment with my wife in bed and the baby sleeping in a drawer. During the day I worked in a fast food joint and three nights a week I bartended. It took 14 months to write, 8 years to get it published, and after the book was released there were four spelling errors the company and I had missed – go figure. Book was reviewed by Publishers Weekly with no mention of spelling.

12) How long does it take to write a novel?

As long as it takes – three months, six months, one year, two years. It is not like baking a cake or frying chicken. I have four books I have been working on for five years.

13) What should I write with?

Some writers write long hand, some like typewriters, some dictate into a recording device, some use a computer, lap top, ipad. Write on butcher paper if you want. Whatever makes you comfortable. It might be hard to comprehend in this modern world but remember, **YOU ARE YOUR OWN BOSS**. I know a writer who writes on yellow pads and will only use red ink pens.

14) Should I correct a book as I write it or wait to the end and then start editing?

The modern rule of thought is to blast it all out and then go back and correct everything. This way you will not lose the main idea of your book. This idea has come about in our modern times since we are all doing about 3,000 miles an hour in our daily lives. Myself, for my first draft, I write each day until I have had enough, stop writing with a dangling thought, normally not finishing a sentence, and then in the morning I know where I am. When I am finished with the book I let it set for two or three months and then go over it again until I can't take it anymore. To complicate matters I normally work on two or three books at a time and do not use an outline but storyboard them as I go. Write your book the way you feel comfortable writing it.

15) How many times should I rewrite my book?

You will know when enough is enough. It is possible to rewrite your book so many times you lose touch with what you wanted to say. If this happens you will get hopelessly lost and chalk it up to practice not a huge waste of time.

16) Do e-books sell more than traditional books?

Since 2015 e-book sales have leveled off and print has made a huge comeback, so much so many of the big publishers have increased their print runs. On an average 70% of all book sales are print.

17) Is self-publishing better than traditional publishing?

They are both a beast but when it comes to exposure and sales traditional still outweighs self-publishing. Like everything in life, there are always exceptions, but they are few and far between.

18) Are book stores on the decline?

No. Contrary to what most writers are told book stores are alive and well, in fact independent bookstores are on the increase. I hear writers and small publishers say, "If I drive people to my own website I can make more money." True, but can you get as much exposure as Barnes and Nobel worldwide. If your book hits can you do a print run of 250,000 copies?

19) What do I need to be a writer?

Something to write with, a dictionary, a word usage book (for example when to use affect and effect, accept and except, toward and towards) and a zillion other weird things that English spelling has done to make English so complicated and the wisdom to know inspiration is fleeting and the rest of the writing process is **WORK**.

20) I received a lousy review and now I am shattered and do not know what to do?

Get over it.

21) Why are there trolls on Amazon that give 1 star reviews and don't even read the book?

If I could answer this question I could also answer the following? Why are there wars? Why is there starvation? Why do we pollute when we know it will kill us? Why have we raped our planet? Why does the United States have a president that is an idiot? Why? Why? Why? Because some people are mean spirited I suppose.

22) Should I write from an outline?

Some do, some don't. I know a writer who puts sketching paper all over a wall and as he writes he writes on the wall what is happening in his story. I know another writer that knows the end of the book in his head and writes to it. I know people who get an idea, start writing, and the story goes where it is going to go. I know a writer that makes such an extensive outline it could be the book.

23) Has Amazon become too big?

Any place that will sell books for the little guy is ok by me. Plus, to post a book is free and they pay every two months. What more do you want? The only thing that would make it better is if they tossed in a hotdog and a beer.

24) A small publisher wants to do a book of mine but they also want me to buy books before publication. They will cover all cost of publication. Should I do it?

This is nothing but a vanity press in disguise. All they are doing is covering their cost and making a profit on you. Keep looking for a publisher or self publish.

25) How many writers are there in the United States?

There is no way of really knowing the exact amount but estimates are over several million. To be on the optimistic side your chances of getting published are far better than your chances of winning the Lotto.

26) Why can't I be normal and be happy with an 8 to 5 job, paid vacation, and a mortgage?

Because being normal with an 8 to 5 job, a paid vacation, and a mortgage is a living hell. You are fortunate to be a writer.

27) Should I join a writing club?

If you want feedback on your work, help when you feel down, like to associate with a like-minded group of people you should. If you are an introvert, like being alone, hate groups, you shouldn't.

28) What gets published and what doesn't?

That is the million dollar question. Some garbage makes it to the market while a truly fantastic book never gets published. I have never been able to answer this question and it has haunted me since I started writing. The majority of time traditional houses publishing fiction fill their lists with books that a person with an attention span of several minutes will read – the time between commercials on a TV show – after that the reader loses interest.

29) Is there any good news about being a writer?

Yes. If you have only sold one book you have enriched or entertained someone's life. You have followed your true passion in life – many do not have the strength or fortitude to follow their passion and let life take them where it will.

30) If you have any other questions you may contact me on my website, Facebook, or e-mail. I will be glad to give my humble opinion.

CHAPTER TWENTY TWO
WHAT MAKES A FICTION BOOK POPULAR

What makes a book popular is an age old mystery. It is not all promotion. I have seen writers put a book on Amazon, do no promotion, have no author page, web page, blog, and the books sells thousands of copies. There have been small press books that come out of nowhere and sell a million copies. Punctuation does not make a book popular, or grammar, sentence structure, length of paragraphs, length of chapters, word count, sentence length, adverbs or adjectives, nouns or pronouns, the development of great characters, or descriptions, or any of the other things experts say makes a good novel. The cover might make you pick up the book but it will not make you keep reading the book. The fact the author gave you a book mark, head band, a tote bag, or a bag of pot when you purchased the book will not make you read the entire book. When I was younger I believed luck and hard work were the secrets to a good book. Hard work does perfect your writing and in all of life there is always of portion of luck, but now I feel books that become popular become so because the reader knows when the author has put their heart and being and blood into the words. The heart and being and blood blend together and become a magical spirit that resides in the words until the reader absorbs them into their inner self. When you become enraptured by a book you have become one with the magic, one with the spirit, one with the blood of the author.

When I go to bookstores I walk the aisles aimlessly and there is always a book that for no apparent reason I am drawn to – many times it is on the bottom shelf below eye level – a cousin to the mop. I think the author's force radiates out to me – more often than not I purchase this book. For e-books I do not worry if 1 person or 287 have reviewed the book. I seldom read reviews. I read the author's bio. If I like the bio I purchase the book.

There is only one reason a book becomes popular. It possesses the author's magic – a magic that is tangible.

TO WRITE YOU MUST READ

CHAPTER TWENTY THREE
IN SUMMARY

There are countless books that will tell you how to write, what to write, when to write, when not to write, how to find an agent, how to write a query letter, how to write a synopsis, how to punctuate, how to spell. We live in a how to world. The only how to you need to know about writing fiction is when you feel it is right it is right. Your mind does not lie to you. You know when something is not working and you know when something is.

NOBODY, NO ONE WRITES THE SAME. NOBODY, NO ONE PUNCTUATES THE SAME. NOBODY, NO ONE WRITES THE SAME LENGTH SENTENCES – THE SAME LENGTH BOOKS – USES THE SAME WORDS TO DESCRIBE SOMETHING – AND ON AND ON. BE YOU.

There is no secret to writing a best seller although there are countless books on how to become either a traditional best seller or an indie best seller. Some books sell a zillion copies that are garbage, some books never get published that are pure literary gems - go figure. For people who say there is no luck I will argue until the day I die there is an enormous amount of luck in the writing game. You cannot give up, work makes its own luck. In the indie book game it is also a lot of work to get your book read. You don't just put it on Amazon or Nook and other sites and start counting your money and people all over the country want your autograph.

Here is a dirty little secret about the New York Times Best Seller List. The books that make the list are the books that sell the most copies for one week – the amount of copies might only be twenty books. It is as deceiving as a person giving away free books saying they sold a certain number of books – people will take almost anything if it is free.

CHAPTER TWENTY FOUR
IN CLOSING

I hope you have been able to glean a few morsels out of this book that will help you in your crazy desire to be a fiction writer. There are many other topics that could be glossed over, feel free to contact me on any subject, but the main thing to remember is to have faith in yourself and trust in your own judgment. Good luck with your writing.

The End

If you enjoyed this book would you please leave a review on your favorite book site and tell ten million people to purchase a copy so my wife and I can move to the Big Island where I would love to open a bookstore that sells only indie books. If you would like to contact me you may leave a comment on my website: swisherbooks.com...e-mail me: swisherwritesfiction@gmail.com... or message me on Facebook.

The best to you and yours:
Robert K. Swisher Jr.

NOTES

NOTES

NOTES

NOTES

www.ingramcontent.com/pod-product-compliance
Lightning Source LLC
Chambersburg PA
CBHW070620300426
44113CB00010B/1600